Prayer Jujit for Vigilant Prayer Warfare

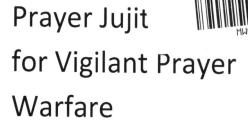

By Rev. Dr. William Hernandez

For my eight arrows who are also my eight treasures.

Thank you to my helper, my bride, for your proofreading and suggestions.

Contents

> "Persevere in prayer, being vigilant in it with thanksgiving" (Colossians 4:2, MOUNCE).

Introduction

Jujitsu is the art of being vigilant and prepared to deflect (or counter) any attack.

My opponent thrust the wooden knife toward my abdomen. I deflected the attack. Then, we repeated the exercise. This was a part of my training in jujitsu at the dojo (martial arts training center) that stood near the edge of my hometown.

In that training center, our group of around 25 students learned lists of moves. These lists hung on the walls around the mat where we practiced. From one list we learned how to escape from various grips. From another list we learned how to throw opponents to the ground. From yet other lists we learned arm locks, submission moves, and how to block weapon attacks. In summary, we learned how to become vigilant and prepared for evading attacks, deflecting attacks, absorbing attacks, and escaping from various attacks. Eventually, I earned an advanced rank.

In the same way that I learned jujitsu and the art of defense, the Scriptures teach us how to be on guard against the attacks of the evil one. God desires for you to be protected from our spiritual enemy's attacks. The attacks of the enemy center on one thing: Destroying your prayer life.

Defining Prayer

One of the words for prayer in Hebrew, *Pagha*, can be translated, "a meeting with an outcome." Moses met with God (See **Isaiah 64:3-5**). God revealed Himself to Moses as **"I AM"** (Heb. *Yahweh*) in **Exodus 3:14**, which emphasized His eternal nature. Jesus used the phrase, "I AM" in reference to Himself in the Gospels. These "I AM" statements are quoted in this devotional to focus our attention on our "meetings" with the Lord.

Christ stated in some of His final words to the Disciples, **"...and lo, I am with you always, even to the end of the age" (Matthew 28:20b, NASB 1977)**. In the Greek text, the flow of thought is, **"I—with you—AM"**. Thus, the "I AM" statements of Christ highlight the essence of our prayer life, our "meeting" with God.

An operational definition for prayer, therefore, is <u>meeting with God through (1) leaning on Him, **"casting all your anxiety on Him, because He cares for you" (1 Peter 5:7, NASB)**, (2) listening to Him, (3) praising Him, and (4) lovingly serving others, as He accepts our love toward others as love toward Himself</u> **(Matthew 25:40)**. These four branches of prayer become the four battlegrounds in prayer warfare.

The Center of the War

Jesus the Messiah taught, **"I am the vine; you are the branches. If you remain in me and I in you, you will bear much fruit; apart from me you can do nothing"** (John 15:5, NIV). The promise of bearing fruit is seeing others come to faith **(Romans 1:13)**. We focus on abiding in Christ that we can **"bear much fruit"** (John 15:5a, NIV). This is a true promise from our Lord. He also says, **"apart from me you can do nothing (John 15:5b, NIV)**. That promise also comes true. Let's stay **"vigilant"** in prayer together **(Colossians 4:2)**. Let's be obsessed with prayer!

Christ taught us to bear fruit among the nations. He said, **"And this gospel of the kingdom will be preached in the whole world as a testimony to all nations, and then the end will come"** (Matthew 24:14, NIV). When the end comes, it will be "game over" for the enemy. He has nothing to look forward to except a lake of fire **(Revelation 20:10)**. The enemy is doing everything he can to try to postpone his coming destruction.

If I were on the enemy's team, I would do everything to hinder the Gospel from getting to the last reached groups on earth. There is a verse that states, **"...Satan blocked the way"** (1 Thessalonians 2:18b, NIV). The meaning of the Greek word translated, "blocked", is that of an army in retreat which, "breaks up the road", thus hindering the pursuing army. That is what Satan is trying to do. But we will pursue. The Good

News of God's forgiveness and new life will reach the last reached groups **(Revelation 5:9)**, even at great sacrifice. These groups deserve to hear the hope of salvation as much as you or I did. We will bear fruit among them. Our Lord taught, **"This kind of spirit can be forced out only by prayer,"** (Mark 9:29, GWT). As we reach the last of the last, Jesus' teaching must be taken seriously.

As we go forward, bringing the message of God's forgiveness and new life to the last of the last people groups on earth, that is, to **"all nations" (Matthew 24:14, NIV)**, there will be an increase in international conflict, **"…wars and rumors of wars" (Matthew 24:6, NIV)**. I am persuaded that this is an attempt to block God's workers from getting access to countries which house the last groups to be reached on earth. I am also persuaded (and have experienced) that there will be an increased level of personal attacks against God's workers and those who help them. These attacks focus on destroying our prayer lives.

To be **truly** willing to pray at all costs, to **truly** persevere in prayer, and **truly** seek only victory in our prayer lives so that the Gospel goes forward to all nations is to put on **"the belt of truth" (Ephesians 6:14, NIV)**, which keeps us from being hindered by the "loose ends" of the clothing of unwillingness in warfare.[1] For

---

[1] John MacArthur, ed., *The MacArthur Study Bible* (Nashville: Thomas Nelson Publishers, 1997), note on Ephesians 6:14.

those who are willing, I welcome you to the battlefield of prayer warfare. I welcome you to vigilantly meet with God and bear fruit among the nations.

War Plan for Meeting with God

The following pages are arranged as a monthly devotional to keep us vigilant about defending our prayer lives throughout the month.

The "Daily Prayer" page is for listing those closest to you, your spiritual children, and people groups closest to your heart.

Following the "Daily Prayer" page, there is a 28-day devotional for the first 28 days of each month. Each day begins with some verses that highlight what may hinder your prayers. There are about sixty ways that our prayers can be hindered according to the Scriptures. As we think through these verses daily, let us be mindful with the Apostle Paul, who said, **"I don't want Satan to outwit us. After all, we are not ignorant about Satan's scheming (2 Corinthians 2:11, GWT)**. As you work through this manual month after month, may prayer and defending your prayer life become as natural and consistent for you as breathing.

Each day also has a page for listing believers and non-believers for whom you are praying. This is also good to remind you to be in touch with those you've listed.

For the first 14 days of the devotional, there are 14 relationships listed. Reflect on these vital relationships and journal your vision and strategies for maintaining these relationships. Reflect on your goals, struggles, and successes in these relationships.

There are listed on the final 14 days of the devotional the last people groups on earth to be reached with the Gospel. These are the most desperate to hear of the hope we have. If you are praying in a group, each person can pray for four people groups at a time. Pray for these groups that God will send them missionaries and that He would prepare their hearts to receive the message of hope.

Finally, the last few pages of the devotional are called "Juice Day Notes." Use these pages when you fast. Write down the thoughts God leads you to ponder.

An operational definition of joy is to know your purpose and to live it. You were designed to be a prayer warrior. There is no greater joy than meeting with God, defending your prayer life, and seeing others come to faith.

Our prayer is that this manual will be a useful tool that gets into the hands of the most strategic of God's people who will fellowship with God in bringing the Gospel to all nations. Our most strategic realm is in encouraging, teaching, and equipping the Body of Christ to pray.

~ Daily Prayers ~

Prayer is a relationship of love

Lord Jesus, we desire Your presence. You promised, "and lo, I am with you always, even to the end of the age" (Matt. 28:20b, NASB).

Turn to Jesus through the "I AM" statements!

"I tell you the truth, before Abraham was even born, I AM!" (John 8:58, NLT).

1) Household & Spiritual Children

-
-
-
-
-
-
-
-
-
-
-
-

2) People groups

-
-

Prayer Battleground One: Vigilance in Serving Others

"Come to me, all you who are weary and burdened, and I will give you rest. Take my yoke upon you and learn from me for I am meek and lowly in heart and you will find rest for your souls, for my yoke is easy and my burden is light" (Matthew 11:28-29, NIV).

Introduction: The Warfare Against Relationships

Jesus the Messiah always loved others. We serve with Him. We never serve alone. Christ taught, "...**whatever you did for the least of these brothers and sisters of mine, you did for me" (Matthew 25:40).** Thus, Christ helps us to love others. Moreover, Christ accepts your love or lack of love toward others as your love or lack of love toward Him.

Satan, in order to block your way from abiding in Christ, desires to keep you in <u>bondage to hatred and neglect in your relationships</u>, that you might not bear fruit. Some of the following verses illustrate bondage to <u>forms of hatred and neglect in our relationships</u>, which hinder our prayers. Others of the following verses demonstrate how to abide in Christ through vigilantly serving others. Take time to reflect on these verses daily so that you can defend your prayer life.

Day 1: Vigilance in Serving Others

Defend your prayer life! Prayers are hindered by...

1. Dishonoring our spouse
   - "In the same way, you husbands must give honor to your wives. Treat your wife with understanding as you live together. She may be weaker than you are, but she is your equal partner in God's gift of new life. Treat her as you should so your prayers will not be hindered" (1 Peter 3:7, NLT).
   - [Speaking of Christ, it was written,] "He will not shout or cry out, or raise his voice in the streets" (Isaiah 42:2, NIV).
   - "And if a woman has a husband who is not a believer and he is willing to live with her, she must not divorce him" (1 Corinthians 7:13, NIV).
2. Not praying with our families
   - "Pour out your wrath...on the families that do not call Your name..." (Jeremiah 10:25a, NASB).

Verbalize your struggles & successes in these areas.

"I am the bread of life. Whoever comes to me will never be hungry again. Whoever believes in me will never be thirsty" (John 6:35, NLT).

1) Daily prayers & prayer for today's schedule

2) Believers *(Names beginning with the letter 'A')*

-
-
-
-
-
-
-
-
-

3) Unbelievers & People Groups

-
-
-
-
-
-
-

Relational Vision & Strategy 1 ~ Spouse

What are your goals, struggles, and successes in this relationship? How are these goals being scheduled?

- **Goals**
-
-
-
-
-
-
-
-
-
-
-
-
- **Struggles**
-
-
-
-
-
-

-
-
-
-
-
-
- **Successes**
-
-
-
-
-
-
-
-
-
-
-
-
-

Pray through your goals and struggles. Rejoice and thank God for your growth and successes!

Day 2: Vigilance in Serving Others

Defend your prayer life! Prayers are hindered by...

3. Preferring traditions rather than mercy
   - **"But you [Pharisees] say it is all right for people to say to their parents, 'Sorry, I can't help you. For I have vowed to give to God what I would have given to you.' In this way you let them disregard their needy parents. And so you cancel the word of God in order to hand down your own traditions. And this is only one example among many others"** (Mark 7:11-13, NLT).
4. Not caring for the poor
   - **"Whoever shuts their ears to the cry of the poor will also cry out and not be answered"** (Proverbs 21:13, NIV).

Verbalize your struggles & successes in these areas.

"I am the light of the world. He who follows Me shall not walk in darkness, but have the light of life" (John 8:12, NKJV).

1) Daily prayers & prayer for today's schedule

2) Believers *(Names beginning with the letter 'B')*

-
-
-
-
-
-
-
-
-

3) Unbelievers & People Groups

-
-
-
-
-
-
-

Relational Vision & Strategy 2 ~ Children

What are your goals, struggles, and successes in these relationships? How are these goals being scheduled?

- **Goals**
-
-
-
-
-
-
-
-
-
-
-
-
-

- **Struggles**
-
-
-
-
-
-

-
-
-
-
-
-
- Successes
-
-
-
-
-
-
-
-
-
-
-
-
-
-

Pray through your goals and struggles. Rejoice and thank God for your growth and successes!

Day 3: Vigilance in Serving Others

Defend your prayer life! Prayers are hindered by...

5. Bitterness, ungodly anger and ungodly speech
   - **"But I tell you that anyone who is angry with a brother or sister will be subject to judgment. If you call someone an idiot, you are in danger of being brought before the court. And if you curse someone, you are in danger of the fires of hell" (Matthew 5:22, NIV & NLT).**

6. Refusing to seek reconciliation
   - **"So if you are presenting a sacrifice at the altar in the Temple and you suddenly remember that someone has something against you, leave your sacrifice there at the altar. Go and be reconciled to that person. Then come and offer your sacrifice to God" (Matthew 5:23, NLT).**

Verbalize your struggles & successes in these areas.

"Yes, I am the gate. Those who come in through me will be saved. They will come and go freely and will find good pastures" (John 10:9, NLT).

1) Daily prayers & prayer for today's schedule

2) Believers *(Names beginning with the letter 'C')*

-
-
-
-
-
-
-
-

3) Unbelievers & People Groups

-
-
-
-
-
-
-
-

Relational Vision & Strategy 3 ~ Parents

What are your goals, struggles, and successes in these relationships? How are these goals being scheduled?

- **Goals**
-
-
-
-
-
-
-
-
-
-
-
-
- **Struggles**
-
-
-
-
-
-

-
-
-
-
-
-
- Successes
-
-
-
-
-
-
-
-
-
-
-
-
-
-

Pray through your goals and struggles. Rejoice
and thank God for your growth and successes!

Day 4: Vigilance in Serving Others

Defend your prayer life! Prayers are hindered by...

7. Overextending oneself and breaking one's word
   - **"Just say a simple, 'Yes, I will,' or 'No, I won't.' Anything beyond this is from the evil one" (Matthew 5:37, NLT).**
8. Lying
   - **"...Pay attention to my prayer, for it comes from honest lips" (Psalm 17:1b, NLT).**

Verbalize your struggles & successes in these areas.

"I am the good shepherd. The good shepherd sacrifices his life for the sheep" (John 10:11, NLT).

1) Daily prayers & prayer for today's schedule

2) Believers *(Names beginning with the letter 'D')*

-
-
-
-
-
-
-
-

3) Unbelievers & People Groups

-
-
-
-
-
-
-
-

Relational Vision & Strategy 4 ~ Distressed Neighbors/Poor

What are your goals, struggles, and successes in these relationships? How are these goals being scheduled?

- **Goals**
-
-
-
-
-
-
-
-
-
-
-
-
-

- **Struggles**
-
-
-
-
-

-
-
-
-
-
-
-
- **Successes**
-
-
-
-
-
-
-
-
-
-
-
-
-
-

Pray through your goals and struggles. Rejoice and thank God for your growth and successes!

Day 5: Vigilance in Serving Others

Defend your prayer life! Prayers are hindered by...

9. Condemnation, judging, and unforgiveness
   - "Be merciful, just as your Father is merciful. Do not judge, and you will not be judged. Do not condemn, and you will not be condemned. Forgive and you will be forgiven" (Luke 6:36, 37, NIV).
10. A spirit of vengeance
    - "You have heard the law that says the punishment must match the injury: 'An eye for an eye, and a tooth for a tooth.' But I say, do not resist an evil person! If someone slaps you on the right cheek, offer the other cheek also" (Matthew 5:39, 40, NLT).
11. Hatred
    - "If your enemy is hungry, give him some food to eat, and if he is thirsty, give him some water to drink. [In this way] you will make him feel guilty and ashamed, and the LORD will reward you" (Proverbs 25:21, 22, GWT).
    - "Whoever claims to love God yet hates a brother or sister is a liar" (1 John 4:20a, NIV).

Verbalize your struggles & successes in these areas.

"I am the resurrection and the life. Anyone who believes in me will live, even after dying. Everyone who lives in me and believes in me will never ever die" (John 11:25, NLT).

1) Daily prayers & prayer for today's schedule

2) Believers *(Names beginning with the letter 'E')*

-
-
-
-
-
-
-
-

3) Unbelievers & People Groups

-
-
-
-
-
-

Relational Vision & Strategy 5 ~ Hospitality to Outsiders

What are your goals, struggles, and successes in these relationships? How are these goals being scheduled?

- **Goals**
-
-
-
-
-
-
-
-
-
-
-
-
- **Struggles**
-
-
-
-
-

-
-
-
-
-
-
-
- Successes
-
-
-
-
-
-
-
-
-
-
-
-
-
-

Pray through your goals and struggles. Rejoice
and thank God for your growth and successes!

Day 6: Vigilance in Serving Others

Defend your prayer life! Prayers are hindered by...

12. Undercommunicating God's ways to others
    - **"Without prophetic vision people run wild, but blessed are those who follow [God's] teachings" (Proverbs 29:18, GWT).**
13. Neglecting to oversee and pastor others
    - **"Be shepherds of God's flock that is under your care, watching over them—not because you must, but because you are willing, as God wants you to be; not pursuing dishonest gain, but eager to serve" (1 Peter 5:2, NIV).**

Verbalize your struggles & successes in these areas.

Turn to Jesus through the "I AM" statements!

"I am the way, the truth, and the life. No one can come to the Father except through me" (John 14:6, NLT).

1) Daily prayers & prayer for today's schedule

2) Believers *(Names beginning with the letter 'F')*

-
-
-
-
-
-
-
-

3) Unbelievers & People Groups

-
-
-
-
-
-
-

Relational Vision & Strategy 6 ~ Temple Maintenance

What are your goals, struggles, and successes for your own health? How are these goals being scheduled?

- Goals
-
-
-
-
-
-
-
-
-
-
-
-
- Struggles
-
-
-
-
-

-
-
-
-
-
-
-
- Successes
-
-
-
-
-
-
-
-
-
-
-
-
-

Pray through your goals and struggles. Rejoice
and thank God for your growth and successes!

Day 7: Vigilance in Serving Others

Defend your prayer life! Prayers are hindered by...

14. A lack of planning to maintain our relationships (Planning ahead helps to avoid chaos. Chaos destroys relationships.)
    - **"a sensible person watches his step." (Proverbs 14:15b, GWT).**
15. Planning our course without seeking God's will
    - **"I know, LORD, that our lives are not our own. We are not able to plan our own course" (Jeremiah 10:23, NLT).**
16. Neglecting all kinds of relationships and not seeking wholeness in them
    - **"Blessed are the peacemakers, for they will be called children of God" (Matthew 5:9, NIV).**

Verbalize your struggles & successes in these areas.

"Yes, I am the vine; you are the branches. Those who remain in me, and I in them, will produce much fruit. For apart from me you can do nothing" (John 15:5, NLT).

1) Daily prayers & prayer for today's schedule

2) Believers *(Names beginning with the letter 'G')*

-
-
-
-
-
-
-
-

3) Unbelievers & People Groups

-
-
-
-
-
-
-

What are your goals, struggles, and successes in relying on Christ through prayer? How are these goals being scheduled?

Be obsessed with prayer. God desires of us to seek Him regularly and consistently, as it is written, **"Pray without ceasing" (1 Thessalonians 5:17, KJV)**. Unfortunately, there is a widespread misunderstanding that being serious about prayer means that you get up very, very early at 3, 4, or 5 am to pray every single day. For some people, very early morning prayer is their favorite way to meet with Jesus, as it is written, **"I rise before dawn and cry for help" (Psalm 119:147a, NIV)**. For many others who attempt this pattern of prayer, it becomes very legalistic and unrealistic. They soon face their own failure and give up entirely on prayer itself. It is so important that our prayer goals be unique and realistic. God knows the specific and individual challenges in each person's life, such as work schedule, infant sleep patterns, health challenges, etc.

Take time below to list your specific goals for meeting with the Lord (answer the questions: Who, what, when, where, how, and why). Then, consider if the goals are realistic given your unique, God-given situation. Remember that Jesus loves variety. Though He desires for us to be obsessed with prayer, He does not call us all to meet with Him in the exact same ways. Even your own patterns of prayer may change with time.

- Goals
-
-
-
-
-
-
-
- Struggles
-
-
-
-
-
-
- Successes
-
-
-
-
-
-

Pray through your goals and struggles. Rejoice and thank God for your growth and successes!

Small Group Summary: The War Plan for Serving Others

To be in right relationship with others is to put on **"love as a breastplate" (Ephesians 6: 14, NIV)** in your war to abide in Christ. The following are some suggestions for improving your relationships with others:

Small Group Activities:

- **Adapt one of the verses above to a humorous skit. Have one person exemplify the good path (or the bad path), and the other person attempt to persuade the first against it.[2]**
- **As a small group, discuss the verses above that have helped you in your prayer life and the verses that challenge you.**

Personal Activities:

- **Make plans to bless your spouse and children. Communicate regularly about these plans with them. Perhaps you can have a weekly coffee date to talk.**
- **Communicate with your parents regularly, which is one way to care for them.**
- **Prayerfully seek one way to bless the poor (only one because you can't do everything).**

---

[2] Sol Stein, *Stein on Writing* (New York: St. Martin's Griffin, 1995), note on role playing.

- **Consider how to better manage your time. Find a couple of ways to improve your time management, such as keeping a journal or calendar or wearing a watch.**

It is a blessing to bring more and more order and peace into our lives. It is written, **"The wisdom of the prudent is to give thought to their ways..." (Proverbs 14:8a, NIV)**. Protect your relationship with Christ through serving others in love and with order.

Prayer Battleground Two: Vigilance in Listening to Christ

"...Mary sat at the Lord's feet and listened to his teaching" (Luke 10:39, ESV).

Introduction: The Warfare Against Listening to our Beloved Savior and King

Christ taught, **"I am the true grapevine, and my Father is the gardener. He cuts off every branch of mine that doesn't produce fruit, and he prunes the branches that do bear fruit so they will produce even more" (John 15:1, 2, NLT)**. Thus, repentance leads us to bearing more fruit among the nations.

Satan, in order to block your way from abiding in Christ, desires to keep you in bondage to <u>ignorance and the disobeying of the Word of Christ</u>, that you might not bear fruit. Some of the following verses illustrate bondage to <u>forms of ignorance and the disobeying of Christ's Words</u>, which hinder our prayers. Others of the following verses demonstrate how to abide in Christ through vigilantly listening to Him.

Take time to reflect on these verses daily so that you can defend your prayer life. Also, see Appendix 1 for a sample Bible study method.

Day 8: Vigilance in Listening to Christ

Defend your prayer life! Prayers are hindered by...

1) Being busy rather than listening to Christ
   - **"But the Lord said to [the sister of Mary], 'My dear Martha, you are worried and upset over all these details!" (Luke 10:41, NLT).**

2) Cherishing sin
   - **"If I had cherished sin in my heart, the Lord would not have listened" (Psalm 66:18, NIV).**

Verbalize your struggles & successes in these areas.

"I am the bread of life. Whoever comes to me will never be hungry again. Whoever believes in me will never be thirsty" (John 6:35, NLT)

1) Daily prayers & prayer for today's schedule

2) Believers *(Names beginning with the letter 'H')*

-
-
-
-
-
-
-
-

3) Unbelievers & People Groups

-
-
-
-
-
-
-
-

Relational Vision & Strategy 8 ~ Leaning on Christ with Others

What are your goals, struggles, and successes in your prayer partner relationships? How are these goals being scheduled?

- **Goals**
-
-
-
-
-
-
-
-
-
-
-
-

- **Struggles**
-
-
-
-

-
-
-
-
-
-
-
- **Successes**
-
-
-
-
-
-
-
-
-
-
-
-

Pray through your goals and struggles. Rejoice and thank God for your growth and successes!

Defend your prayer life! Prayers are hindered by...

3) Disobeying God's commandments
   - "[We] receive from Him anything we ask, because we keep his commands and do what pleases Him" (1 John 3:22, NIV).

4) Self-righteousness
   - [First, a self-righteous person prayed at the Temple,] "But the tax collector stood at a distance. He would not even look up to heaven, but beat his breast and said, 'God have mercy on me, a sinner.' I tell you that this man, rather than the other [self-righteous person], went home justified before God. For all those who exalt themselves will be humbled, and those who humble themselves will be exalted" (Luke 18:13, 14, NIV).

Verbalize your struggles & successes in these areas.

"I am the light of the world. He who follows Me shall not walk in darkness, but have the light of life" (John 8:12, NKJV).

1) Daily prayers & prayer for today's schedule

2) Believers *(Names beginning with the letter 'I')*

-
-
-
-
-
-
-
-
-

3) Unbelievers & People Groups

-
-
-
-
-
-
-

Relational Vision & Strategy 9 ~ Fasting

What are your goals, struggles, and successes in this area? How are these goals being scheduled?

- Goals
-
-
-
-
-
-
-
-
-
-
-
-

- Struggles
-
-
-
-
-
-

-
-
-
-
-
-
- Successes
-
-
-
-
-
-
-
-
-
-
-
-
-
-
-

Pray through your goals and struggles. Rejoice
and thank God for your growth and successes!

Day 10: Vigilance in Listening to Christ

Defend your prayer life! Prayers are hindered by...

5) Wrong motives.
   - **"When you ask, you do not receive, because you ask with wrong motives, that you may spend what you get on your pleasures" (James 4:3, NIV).**

6) Ignorance of God's will
   - **"This is the confidence we have in approaching God: That if we ask anything according to His will, he hears us" (1 John 5:14, NIV).**

Verbalize your struggles & successes in these areas.

"Yes, I am the gate. Those who come in through me will be saved. They will come and go freely and will find good pastures" (John 10:9, NLT).

1) Daily prayers & prayer for today's schedule

2) Believers *(Names beginning with the letter 'J')*

-
-
-
-
-
-
-
-
-

3) Unbelievers & People Groups

-
-
-
-
-
-
-

Relational Vision & Strategy 10 ~ Listening to Christ

What are your goals, struggles, and successes in listening to the Word of God? How are these goals being scheduled? (See Appendix 1 for a sample Bible study).

- **Goals**
-
-
-
-
-
-
-
-
-
-
-

- **Struggles**
-
-
-
-

-
-
-
-
-
-
-
-
- Successes
-
-
-
-
-
-
-
-
-
-
-

Pray through your goals and struggles. Rejoice and thank God for your growth and successes!

Day 11: Vigilance in Listening to Christ

Defend your prayer life! Prayers are hindered by...

7) Misrepresenting God
   - "My servant Job will pray for you, and I will accept his prayer on your behalf. I will not treat you as you deserve, for you have not spoken accurately about me, as my servant Job has," (Job 42:8b, NLT).

8) Not sharing the Scriptures
   - "The Spirit of the Lord speaks through me; his Words are upon my tongue," (2 Samuel 23:2, NLT).

9) Not giving nor receiving godly counsel
   - "Timely advice is lovely, like golden apples in a silver basket," (Proverbs 25:11, NLT).
   - "Plans fail for lack of counsel, but with many advisers they succeed" (Proverbs 14:22, NIV).

Verbalize your struggles & successes in these areas.

"I am the good shepherd. The good shepherd sacrifices his life for the sheep" (John 10:11, NLT).

1) Daily prayers & prayer for today's schedule

2) Believers *(Names beginning with the letter 'K')*

-
-
-
-
-
-
-
-
-

3) Unbelievers & People Groups

-
-
-
-
-
-
-
-

What are your goals, struggles, and successes in these relationships? How are these goals being scheduled?

- **Goals**
  -
  -
  -
  -
  -
  -
  -
  -
  -
  -
  -
  -
  -
- **Struggles**
  -
  -
  -
  -
  -

-
-
-
-
-
-
-
- Successes
-
-
-
-
-
-
-
-
-
-
-
-
-

Pray through your goals and struggles. Rejoice and thank God for your growth and successes!

Day 12: Vigilance in Listening to Christ

Defend your prayer life! Prayers are hindered by...

10) Not testing other's counsel against the Word of God

- **"...do not despise prophetic utterances, But examine everything carefully; hold fast to that which is good (1 Thessalonians 5:20, 21, NASB).**

11) Not warning others of the wrong path and hell

- **"When I say to a wicked person, 'You will surely die,' and you do not warn them or speak out to dissuade them from their evil ways in order to save their life, that person will die for their sin, and I will hold you accountable for their blood" (Ezekiel 3:18, NIV).**

Verbalize your struggles & successes in these areas.

"I am the resurrection and the life. Anyone who believes in me will live, even after dying. Everyone who lives in me and believes in me will never ever die" (John 11:25, NLT).

1) Daily prayers & prayer for today's schedule

2) Believers *(Names beginning with the letter 'L')*

-
-
-
-
-
-
-
-
-

3) Unbelievers & People Groups

-
-
-
-
-
-

Relational Vision & Strategy 12 ~ Thanksgiving

What are your goals, struggles, and successes in this area? How are these goals being scheduled?

- ## Goals
-
-
-
-
-
-
-
-
-
-
-
-
-

- ## Struggles
-
-
-
-
-
-
-

-
-
-
-
-
-
- Successes
-
-
-
-
-
-
-
-
-
-
-
-
-
-
-

Pray through your goals and struggles. Rejoice and thank God for your growth and successes!

Day 13: Vigilance in Listening to Christ

Defend your prayer life! Prayers are hindered by...

12) Not encouraging others
- "He makes the whole body fit together perfectly. As each part does its own special work, it helps the other parts grow, so that the whole body is healthy and growing and full of love" (Ephesians 4:16, NLT).

13) Not restraining one's speech
- [There is] "A time to be quiet and a time to speak" (Ecclesiastes 3:7b, NLT).
- "Therefore the prudent keep quiet in such times, for the times are evil" (Amos 5:13, NIV).
- "Don't waste what is holy on people who are unholy. Don't throw your pearls to pigs! They will trample the pearls, then turn and attack you" (Matthew 7:6, NLT).

Verbalize your struggles & successes in these areas.

Turn to Jesus through the "I AM" statements!

"I am the way, the truth, and the life. No one can come to the Father except through me" (John 14:6, NLT).

1) Daily prayers & prayer for today's schedule

2) Believers *(Names beginning with the letter 'M')*

-
-
-
-
-
-
-
-
-

3) Unbelievers & People Groups

-
-
-
-
-
-
-

Relational Vision & Strategy 13 ~ Worshiping God Together

What are your goals, struggles, and successes in this area? How are these goals being scheduled?

- **Goals**
-
-
-
-
-
-
-
-
-
-
-
-

- **Struggles**
-
-
-
-
-
-

-
-
-
-
-
-
-
- Successes
-
-
-
-
-
-
-
-
-
-
-
-
-

Pray through your goals and struggles. Rejoice and thank God for your growth and successes!

Day 14: Vigilance in Listening to Christ

Defend your prayer life! Prayers are hindered by...

14) Not being moved by God
- **"The Holy Spirit said to Philip, 'Go over and walk along beside the carriage" (Acts 8:29, NLT).**

15) Not following one's calling
- **"The LORD gave this message to Jonah son of Amittai, 'Get up and go to the great city of Ninevah" (Jonah 1:1, 2a, NLT).**

Verbalize your struggles & successes in these areas.

"Yes, I am the vine; you are the branches. Those who remain in me, and I in them, will produce much fruit. For apart from me you can do nothing" (John 15:5, NLT).

1) Daily prayers & prayer for today's schedule

2) Believers *(Names beginning with the letter 'N')*

-
-
-
-
-
-
-
-
-

3) Unbelievers & People Groups

-
-
-
-
-

Relational Vision & Strategy 14 ~ "Add to Your Faith Heroic Deeds" (2 Peter 1:5)
As we are yoked with Christ, who lived heroically, we are called to live heroically. What are your goals, struggles, and successes in this area? How are these goals being scheduled?

- Goals
-
-
-
-
-
-
-
-
-
-
-
-
- Struggles
-
-
-
-

-
-
-
-
-
-
-
-
- Successes
-
-
-
-
-
-
-
-
-
-
-
-

Pray through your goals and struggles. Rejoice and thank God for your growth and successes!

Small Group Summary: The War Plan for Listening to our Beloved Savior and King

To listen to your Beloved Savior and King and obey Him is to defensively handle **"the sword of the Spirit, which is the word of God" (Ephesians 6:17, NIV)** in your war to abide in Christ. The following are some suggestions for listening to our Beloved:

Small Group Activities:

- Adapt one of the verses above to a humorous skit. Have one person exemplify the good path, and the other person attempt to persuade the first against the good path.
- As a small group, discuss the verses above that have helped you in your prayer life and the verses that challenge you.

Personal Activities:

- Read a passage of Scripture daily (around 10 verses long). Perhaps you can pair this with a cup of coffee. Highlight things you like, such as God's power, His love, and the good path.
- Re-read the same passage and look for areas about which you need to change your heart and mind. Note places where you need to change your attitudes, beliefs, or actions.

- **Try writing down on an index card a verse you want to memorize. Practice reciting the verse until you can recite it from memory.**

We also model for others listening to our Beloved Savior and King. In doing so, we are a benefit to them, as Paul wrote, **"Whatever you have learned or received or heard from me, or seen in me—put it into practice. And the God of peace will be with you" (Philippians 4:9, NIV).** Proverbs adds, **"Whoever heeds discipline shows the way of life, but whoever ignores correction leads others astray" (Proverbs 10:17, NIV).** Protect your relationship with Christ through listening to His voice.

Prayer Battleground Three: Vigilance in Praise

"But thou art holy, O thou that inhabitest the praises of Israel" (Psalm 22:3, KJV).

Introduction: The Warfare Against Thanksgiving

It is written that the Lord, **"inhabits"** the praises of His people **(Psalm 22:3)**.

Satan, in order to block your way from abiding in Christ, desires to keep you in bondage to discontentment and complaining, that you might not bear fruit. Some of the following verses illustrate bondage to forms of discontentment or complaining, which hinder your prayers. Others of the following verses demonstrate how to abide in Christ through vigilantly Praising God. Take time to reflect on these verses daily so that you can defend your prayer life.

During the last 14 days of the month, we have a focus on the last reached people groups. The "last of the last" people groups to be reached are called "level zero" groups. This means they have no Bible translation in progress nor do they have anyone working to reach them. According to www.peoplegroups.org, there are about 586 of these "last of the last" to be reached. These are listed below.

Pray for (1) receptive hearts, (2) missionaries to be sent, and (3) Bible translations to be started. From slavery in Egypt **(Exodus 3:9)** to the first days of the church **(Acts 1:14)** to modern revivals, it is clear that redemptive movements of God are preceded by vigilant prayer movements of His people. Though God's workers may be the tip of an arrow that goes to dark places, your prayers are the bowstring and God is the Archer.

Though the following statistics were taken from www.peoplegroups.org recently, visit the website to see the progress of reaching these groups and other people groups.

www.peoplegroups.org has brilliantly arranged these people groups by country, people group name, and population. A more detailed description of each people group (including maps of their locations and ethnographical research data) can be found at www.ethnologue.com .

Day 15: Vigilance in Praise

Defend your prayer life! Prayers are hindered by...

1. Complaining (Job modeled for us a path of praising God even in the midst of great loss.)
   - "[and Job] **said, "Naked I came from my mother's womb, and naked I will depart. The LORD gave and the LORD has taken away; may the name of the LORD be praised" (Job 1:21, NIV)**
2. Not enduring amidst persecution (Paul and Silas modeled for us a path of praising God even in the midst of great pain.)
   - [After the two believers were flogged and jailed, it says that,] **"About midnight Paul and Silas were praying and singing hymns to God, and the other prisoners were listening to them" (Acts 16:25, NIV).**

Verbalize your struggles & successes in these areas.

"I am the bread of life. Whoever comes to me will never be hungry again. Whoever believes in me will never be thirsty" (John 6:35, NLT)

1) Daily prayers & prayer for today's schedule

2) Believers *(Names beginning with the letter 'O')*

-
-
-
-
-
-
-
-
-
-

3) Unbelievers & People Groups

-
-
-
-
-
-
-

Last People Groups to Be Reached with Hope

CountryName	PeopleGroup	Population
Afghanistan	Deaf Afghans	119000
Afghanistan	Judeo-Persian Jews	11842
Afghanistan	Moghol	6608
Afghanistan	Pahlavani	3378
Afghanistan	Parya	2056
Albania	Deaf Albanians	16743
Algeria	Berber, Gourara	44627
Algeria	Berber, Tidikelt	16160
Algeria	Berber, Tuat	68680
Algeria	Chenoua	81810
Algeria	Deaf Algerians	222000
Angola	Deaf Angolans	63400
Argentina	Deaf Argentines	228396
Argentina	Tehuelche	200
Armenia	Deaf Armenians	16200
Azerbaijan	Budukh	6146
Azerbaijan	Deaf Azerbaijanis	31000
Azerbaijan	Khinalug	2162
Azerbaijan	Kryz	8877
Azerbaijan	Yergyuch	1138
Bahrain	Deaf Bahrainis	3754
Bangladesh	Koda	1616
Barbados	Deaf Barbadians	1257
Belize	Deaf Belizeans	1531
Benin	Bulba	1828
Benin	Deaf Beninese	34407
Bhutan	Deaf Bhutanese	12044

Bosnia & Herzegovina	Deaf Bosnians	17124
Botswana	Deaf Motswana	8142
Brazil	Akurio	10
Brazil	Amondawa	100
Brazil	Arapaso	537
Brazil	Arutani	17
Brazil	Ava-Canoeiro	17
Brazil	Aweti	171
Brazil	Catawishi	10
Brazil	EnawenÃª-NawÃª	527
Brazil	Guato	700
Brazil	Himarima	80
Brazil	Iapama	200
Brazil	Itogapuk	100
Brazil	Kabixi	100
Brazil	Kashuyana	500
Brazil	Katukina-JutaÃ	600

Day 16: Vigilance in Praise

Defend your prayer life! Prayers are hindered by...

3. Ritualistic worship instead of heartfelt thanksgiving
    - **"Make thankfulness your sacrifice to God and keep the vows you made to the Most High. Then call on Me when you are in trouble and I will rescue you, and you will give me glory" (Psalm 50:14, 15, NLT).**
4. Fear (Daniel modeled for us a path of praising God even in the midst of being threatened.)
    - **"But when Daniel learned that the law [threatening his life] had been signed, he went home and knelt down as usual in his upstairs room, with its windows open toward Jerusalem. He prayed three times a day, just as he had always done, giving thanks to his God" (Daniel 6:10, NLT).**
5. Forgetting God's mercies
    - **"One of them [the ten lepers who were healed], when he saw he was healed, came back, praising God in a loud voice. He threw himself at Jesus' feet and thanked him-and he was a Samaritan. Jesus asked, 'Were not all ten cleansed? Where are the other nine?'" (Luke 17:15-17, NIV).**

Verbalize your struggles & successes in these areas.

"I am the light of the world. He who follows Me shall not walk in darkness, but have the light of life" (John 8:12, NKJV).

1) Daily prayers & prayer for today's schedule

2) Believers *(Names beginning with the letter 'P')*

-
-
-
-
-
-
-
-
-

3) Unbelievers & People Groups

-
-
-
-
-
-
-

Last People Groups to Be Reached with Hope

Brazil	Korubo	500
Brazil	Kreye	30
Brazil	Mandawaka	24
Brazil	Matipuhy-Nahukua	119
Brazil	Miriti-Tapuia	120
Brazil	Morerebi	100
Brazil	Pokanga	165
Brazil	Sabanes	180
Brazil	Sakirabia	103
Brazil	Saluma	300
Brazil	Sikiana	33
Brazil	Tapirape	601
Brazil	Trumai	198
Brazil	Txikao	402
Brazil	Uncontacted of Bararati	21
Brazil	" " of Cumina	21
Brazil	" " of Curuca	20
Brazil	Uncontacted of Igarapã© Tabocal	21
Brazil	Uncontacted of Jandiatuba	300
Brazil	Uncontacted of Madeirinha	21
Brazil	Uncontacted of Mapuera	21
Brazil	Uncontacted of Parauari	21
Brazil	Uncontacted of Quixito	200

Brazil	Uncontacted of Rio Candeias	21
Brazil	Uncontacted of Rio Liberdade	21
Brazil	Uncontacted of Rio TapirapÃ©	21
Brazil	Uncontacted of Sao Jose	300
Brazil	Uncontacted of Serra do Taquaral	50
Brazil	Uncontacted of Teles Pires	21
Brazil	Uraparaquara	100
Brazil	Uru-Pa-In	200
Brazil	Wayoro	77
Brazil	Wokarangma	31
Brazil	Xeta	86
Brazil	Zoe	421
Brunei	Deaf Bruneians	2003
Brunei	Tutung	9000
Bulgaria	Deaf Bulgarians	37185
Burkina Faso	Deaf Burkinabes	55293

Day 17: Vigilance in Praise

Defend your prayer life! Prayers are hindered by...

6. An unrepentant heart (Jonah modeled for us praising God in the midst of repentance.)

   - [Jonah prayed while in the fish,] **"As my life was slipping away, I remembered the LORD. And my earnest prayer went out to you in your holy temple. Those who worship false gods turn their backs on all God's mercies, But I with the voice of thanksgiving will sacrifice to you; what I have vowed I will pay. Salvation belongs to the LORD!" (Jonah 2:7-9, NLT & ESV).**

7. Choosing sin over revering God (Joseph modeled for us a path of remembering and praising God in the midst of temptation.)

   - **"...'with me in change,' [Joseph] told [the wife of Potiphar], 'my master does not concern himself with anything in the house, everything he owns he has entrusted to my care. No one is greater in this house than I am. My master has withheld nothing from me except you, because you are his wife. How then could I do such a wicked thing and sin against God?'" (Genesis 39: 8, 9, NIV).**

Verbalize your struggles & successes in these areas.

"Yes, I am the gate. Those who come in through me will be saved. They will come and go freely and will find good pastures" (John 10:9, NLT).

1) Daily prayers & prayer for today's schedule

2) Believers *(Names beginning with the letter 'Q & R')*

-
-
-
-
-
-
-
-
-

3) Unbelievers & People Groups

-
-
-
-
-
-
-

Last People Groups to Be Reached with Hope

Burundi	Deaf Burundians	37190
Cambodia	Deaf Cambodians	73565
Cameroon	Baldamu	234
Cameroon	Beezen	637
Cameroon	Bomwali	6452
Cameroon	Deaf Cameroonians	70567
Cameroon	Dimbong	149
Cameroon	Dumbule	106
Cameroon	Hijuk	606
Cameroon	Jina	4921
Cameroon	Majera	3281
Cameroon	Ndemli	7546
Cameroon	Pam	76
Canada	Brunei	4761
Canada	Grenadian	9846
Canada	Kutenai	321
Canada	Pentlatch	52
Canada	Saint Vincentian	10721
Canada	West Indian Blacks	7526
Cape Verde	Deaf Cape Verdeans	2308
Central African Republic	Benkonjo	2746
Central African Republic	Deaf Central Africans	19075
Central African Republic	Geme	755

Chad	Amdang	63675
Chad	Baxa	1711
Chad	Berguid	11037
Chad	Bernde	7087
Chad	Bolgo Durag	2283
Chad	Bon Gula	1522
Chad	Boor	249
Chad	Buso	62
Chad	Dama	2630
Chad	Deaf Chadians	51939
Chad	Fanya	1395

Day 18: Vigilance in Praise

Defend your prayer life! Prayers are hindered by…

8. Preferring worldliness rather than delighting in God's teachings
   - **"Rather he delights in the teachings of the LORD and reflects on his teachings day and night" (Psalm 1:2, GWT).**
9. Avoiding God's Word
   - **Let the Word of Christ dwell in you richly, teaching and admonishing one another in all wisdom, singing Psalms and hymns and spiritual songs, with thankfulness in your hearts to God" (Colossians 3:16, ESV).**

Verbalize your struggles & successes in these areas.

"I am the good shepherd. The good shepherd sacrifices his life for the sheep" (John 10:11, NLT).

1) Daily prayers & prayer for today's schedule

2) Believers *(Names beginning with the letter 'S')*

-
-
-
-
-
-
-
-
-

3) Unbelievers & People Groups

-
-
-
-
-
-
-
-

Last People Groups to Be Reached with Hope

Chad	Fongoro	1384
Chad	Goundo	33
Chad	Gula	13063
Chad	Jaya	3205
Chad	Jegu	1865
Chad	Kajakse	14002
Chad	Karanga	12434
Chad	Kendeje	1426
Chad	Koke	892
Chad	Kujarge	1384
Chad	Majera	2749
Chad	Marfa	185349
Chad	Maslam	837
Chad	Mawa	8098
Chad	Mesmedje	32328
Chad	Mimi	11783
Chad	Mogum	8704
Chad	Mubi	43891
Chad	Surbakhal	6921
Chad	Tana	30805
Chad	Torom	10729
Chad	Ubi	1368
Chad	Vale	773
Chile	Deaf Chileans	62946
China	Ai-Cham	3340
China	Ainu	8281
China	Angku	8038
China	A'ou	2345
China	Baima	17443

China	Bit	760
China	Bonan	12056
China	Bugan	3813
China	Buyang	3634
China	De'ang, Shwe	6901
China	Dianbao	11586
China	E	36548
China	Enipu	20868
China	Ga Mong	56950
China	Gepo, Western	8300
China	Guaigun	522
China	Hagei	2663
China	Hu	1662
China	Kemei	1435
China	Kong Ge	1573
China	Lalu, Xuzhang	5217
China	Lalu, Yangliu	48225
China	Lati	2462
China	Linghua	25005
China	Lolo, Southeastern	45808
China	Luzu	1248

Day 19: Vigilance in Praise

Defend your prayer life! Prayers are hindered by...

10. Valuing our enemies' opinions above our Creator

    - **"Yet you have forgotten the LORD, your Creator, the one who stretched out the sky like a canopy and laid the foundations of the earth. Will you remain in constant dread of human oppressors? Will you continue to fear the anger of your enemies? Where is their fury and anger now? It is gone!" (Isaiah 51:13, NLT).**

11. Doubting instead of trusting in God's proven character

    - **"But he must ask in faith without any doubting, for the one who doubts is like the surf of the sea, driven and tossed by the wind" (James 1:6, NASB).**

Verbalize your struggles & successes in these areas.

"I am the resurrection and the life. Anyone who believes in me will live, even after dying. Everyone who lives in me and believes in me will never ever die" (John 11:25, NLT).

1) Daily prayers & prayer for today's schedule

2) Believers *(Names beginning with the letter 'T')*

-
-
-
-
-
-
-
-
-

3) Unbelievers & People Groups

-
-
-
-
-
-

Last People Groups to Be Reached with Hope

China	Manyak	2332
China	Menia	1412
China	Micha	1188
China	Mili	29903
China	Monba, Cona	41326
China	Mozhihei	5297
China	Pengzi	297
China	Popei	5959
China	Suan	297
China	Tajik, Sarikoli	41404
China	Teleut	65
China	Tuerke	215
China	Wunai	11573
China	Xi	1428
China	Yerong	620
China	Yongchun	14715
Colombia	Cabiyari	277
Colombia	Carabayo	300
Colombia	Eastern Tunebo	300
Colombia	Embera-Baudo	5000
Colombia	Macaguan	542
Colombia	Playero	150
Colombia	Tunebo, Angosturas	50
Colombia	Yari	700
Comoros	Deaf Comorans	3524
Congo	Deaf Congolese	17243
Congo	Mbangwe	2111
Congo	Minduumo	4637

Congo	Ngondi	3750
Congo, DRC	Deaf Congolese	343179
Congo, DRC	Koguru	6740
Congo, DRC	Lonzo	453
Congo, DRC	Ndobo	14032
Congo, DRC	Ndunga	5415
Congo, DRC	Ngbinda	7636
Congo, DRC	Ngundu	7636
Congo, DRC	Pelende	10869
Congo, DRC	Samba	5434
Congo, DRC	Seba	241493
Congo, DRC	Sere	9399
Congo, DRC	Songora	4993
Congo, DRC	Tagbo	30839
Congo, DRC	Yakoma	14685
Congo, DRC	Yamongeri	22762

Day 20: Vigilance in Praise

Defend your prayer life! Prayers are hindered by...

12. Complaining when serving God
    - "...serve the LORD your God with joy and enthusiasm for the abundant benefits you have received" (Deuteronomy 28:47b, NLT).
    - "If you do not [serve God in this way]...you will serve your enemies whom the LORD will send against you..." (Deuteronomy 28:47a, 48a NLT).
13. Devaluing Christ, viewing Him as commonplace
    - "Again the Kingdom of Heaven is like a merchant looking for fine pearls. When he found one of great value, he went away and sold everything he had and bought it" (Matthew 13:45, 46, NIV).

Verbalize your struggles & successes in these areas.

"I am the way, the truth, and the life. No one can come to the Father except through me" (John 14:6, NLT).

1) Daily prayers & prayer for today's schedule

2) Believers *(Names beginning with the letter 'U & V')*

-
-
-
-
-
-
-
-
-

3) Unbelievers & People Groups

-
-
-
-
-
-

Last People Groups to Be Reached with Hope

Congo, DRC	Yela	48569
Congo, DRC	Yulu-Binga	734
Cote d'Ivoire	Deaf Ivorians	87151
Cote d'Ivoire	Komono	6468
Cote d'Ivoire	Konyanke	16487
Croatia	Deaf Croatians	17294
Cuba	Deaf Cubans	54237
Cyprus	Deaf Cypriots	3933
Denmark	Danish Travellers	3155
Denmark	Deaf Danish	24400
Djibouti	Deaf Djiboutians	3609
Egypt	Berber, Siwa	12434
Equatorial Guinea	Deaf Equatoguineans	3002
Equatorial Guinea	Yasa	1131
Eritrea	Deaf Eritreans	25519
Eritrea	Nara	97399
Estonia	Deaf Estonians	6292
Ethiopia	Anfillo	1642
Ethiopia	Baiso	1493
Ethiopia	Bale	7001
Ethiopia	Begi-Mao	50224
Ethiopia	Deaf Ethiopians	390042
Ethiopia	Dorze	65515
Ethiopia	Ganza	8058
Ethiopia	Kachama	698
Ethiopia	Karo	1689
Ethiopia	Langa	5834
Ethiopia	Maji	41970

Ethiopia	Melo	119391
Ethiopia	Mesmes	15403
Ethiopia	Nara	61331
Ethiopia	Northern Mao	11339
Ethiopia	Seze	4201
Ethiopia	Shanquilla	31
Ethiopia	Tabi	3452
Ethiopia	Xamir	208775
Ethiopia	Yidinit	700
Fiji	Deaf Fijians	3661
French Guiana	Deaf Guyanese	965
Gabon	Barama	7917

Day 21: Vigilance in Praise

Defend your prayer life! Prayers are hindered by...

14. Not sharing God's mercy in order to safeguard one's own life
    - **"Because thy lovingkindness is better than life, my lips shall praise thee" (Psalm 63:3, KJV).**
15. Valuing family above God
    - **"For God so loved the world that he gave his one and only Son..." (John 3:16a, NIV).**
16. Valuing money above God
    - **"'Bring one-tenth of your income into the storehouse so that there may be food in my house. Test me in this way,' says the LORD of Armies. 'See if I won't open the windows of heaven for you and flood you with blessings'" (Malachi 3:10, GWT).**

Verbalize your struggles & successes in these areas.

"Yes, I am the vine; you are the branches. Those who remain in me, and I in them, will produce much fruit. For apart from me you can do nothing" (John 15:5, NLT).

1) Daily prayers & prayer for today's schedule

2) Believers *(Names beginning with the letter 'W & X')*

-
-
-
-
-
-
-
-
-

3) Unbelievers & People Groups

-
-
-
-
-
-

Last People Groups to Be Reached with Hope

Gabon	Deaf Gabonese	6631
Gabon	Minduumo	5466
Gabon	Northern Teke	19911
Gabon	Simba	4731
Georgia	Deaf Georgians	16834
Ghana	Kantosi	2590
Greece	Deaf Greeks	62695
Guinea	Deaf Guineans	27079
Guinea-Bissau	Deaf Guinea-Bissauans	8023
Iceland	Deaf Icelanders	1384
India	Gadaria (Vaghri)	1714
India	Kahar (Shekhawati)	31403
India	Kandera	25425
India	Kudiya	3914
Indonesia	Bonerate	13000
Indonesia	Campalagian	66000
Indonesia	Deaf Indonesians	1057130
Indonesia	Dondo	13000
Indonesia	Geser Gorom	32000
Indonesia	Hitu	16000
Indonesia	Kluet	50000
Indonesia	Makian Barat	40000
Indonesia	Makian Timur	30000
Indonesia	Patani-Maba	6000
Indonesia	Petapa	569
Indonesia	Seit-Kaitetu	12000
Indonesia	Sula	80000
Indonesia	Taluki	569

Indonesia	Tombelala	1252
Indonesia	Topoiyo	2276
Indonesia	Waru	455
Indonesia	Wawonii	27500
Iran	Alviri-Vidari	1000
Iran	Astiani	20300
Iran	Bashkardi	6000
Iran	Deaf Iranians	349643
Iran	Fars	6763
Iran	Gabri	12000
Iran	Gazi	6000
Iran	Gurani Kurd	26000
Iran	Hulaula	300
Iran	Karingani	17580
Iran	Khalaj	40500

Small Group Summary: The War Plan for Praising our Beloved Savior and King

To praise and thank God, even amidst hardship, is to put on **"the hope of salvation as a helmet" (1 Thessalonians 5:8, NIV)** in your war to abide in Christ. Here are suggestions for praising our Beloved Savior and King.

Small Group Activities:

- **Adapt one of the verses above to a humorous skit. Have one person exemplify the good path, and the other person attempt to persuade the first against the good path.**
- **As a small group, discuss the verses above that have helped you in your prayer life and the verses that challenge you.**

Personal Activities:

- **Set aside a time to write (or think about) what you are thankful for. Perhaps you can pair this with a second cup of coffee in the afternoon.**
- **Find a time to sing praises to God. Experiment with various formats of praise, such as listening to a CD, singing with a hymnal, etc.**
- **Take the Lord's Supper with others regularly.**

Remember the promise Christ taught us about rejoicing. He said, **"Blessed are you when men cast insults at you, and persecute you, and say all kinds of evil** against you falsely on account of me. Rejoice, and be glad, for your reward in heaven is great, for so they persecuted the prophets who were before you" (Matthew 5:11, 12, NASB 1977). Protect your relationship with Christ through praising God amidst any circumstance.

Prayer Battleground Four: Vigilance in Leaning on our Beloved Savior and King

"Who is this coming up from the wilderness leaning on her beloved?" (Song of Solomon 8:5a, NIV).

Introduction: The Warfare Against Leaning on our Beloved Savior and King

Christ taught, **"I am the vine; you are the branches. If you remain in me and I in you, you will bear much fruit; apart from me you can do nothing" (John 15:5, NIV)**. Thus, the time you spend leaning on Christ amidst hardship is the center of your prayer life.

Satan, in order to block your way of abiding in Christ, desires to keep you in bondage to neglecting your relationship with Christ, that you might not bear fruit. Some of following verses illustrate bondage to forms of neglecting your relationship with Christ, which hinders our prayers. Others of the following verses demonstrate how to abide in Christ through vigilantly leaning on Him. Take time to reflect on these verses daily so that you can defend your prayer life.

Day 22: Vigilance in Leaning on Christ

Defend your prayer life! Prayers are hindered by...

1) Viewing prayer as a duty rather than a relationship of love
    - **"But I have this complaint against you. You don't love me or each other as you did at first (Revelation 2:4, NLT).**
    - **"But I am afraid that just as Eve was deceived by the serpent's cunning, your minds may somehow be led astray from your sincere and pure devotion to Christ" (2 Corinthians 11:3, NIV).**
2) Preferring worldliness rather than Christ's presence
    - [Jesus said,] **"Look! I stand at the door and knock. If you hear my voice and open the door, I will come in, and we will share a meal together as friends" (Revelation 3:20, NLT).**
    - **"You will seek me and find me when you seek me with all your heart" (Jeremiah 29:13, NIV).**

Verbalize your struggles & successes in these areas.

"I am the bread of life. Whoever comes to me will never be hungry again. Whoever believes in me will never be thirsty" (John 6:35, NLT)

1) Daily prayers & prayer for today's schedule

2) Believers *(Names beginning with the letter 'Y & Z')*

-
-
-
-
-
-
-
-
-

3) Unbelievers & People Groups

-
-
-
-
-
-
-

Last People Groups to Be Reached with Hope

Iran	Khunsari	20300
Iran	Koroshi	1000
Iran	Mussulman Tat	10100
Iran	Natanzi	6700
Iran	Nayini	6700
Iran	Rudbari	500
Iran	Sangisari	16500
Iran	Semnani	30000
Iran	Senaya	57
Iran	Shahmirzadi	6000
Iran	Shahrudi	1000
Iran	Sivandi	6700
Iran	Soi	6700
Iran	Taromi, Upper	1000
Iran	Vafsi	20300
Iraq	Bajelan	34049
Iraq	Deaf Iraqis	189183
Iraq	Hawrami	32308
Iraq	Koi-sanjaq Sooret	1362
Iraq	Luri	114063
Ireland	Deaf Irish	20662
Ireland	Irish Travellers	6030
Israel	Deaf Israelis	38669
Israel	Hula Hula	10243
Italy	Cimbrian	2230
Italy	Deaf Italians	278400
Italy	Dolomite	30000
Italy	Mocheno	1900
Italy	Walser	3400

Jamaica	Deaf Jamaicans	13560
Jordan	Deaf Jordanians	31927
Kazakhstan	Ili Turki	120
Kazakhstan	Bukharic Jews	800
Kuwait	Deaf Kuwaitis	12219
Kyrgyzstan	Bukharic Jews	455
Laos	Bit	1964
Laos	Bo	3816
Laos	Chut	1591
Laos	Deaf Laotians	29161
Laos	Halang Doan	2300

Day 23: Vigilance in Leaning on Christ

Defend your prayer life! Prayers are hindered by...

3) Being a religious actor rather than Christ's dear friend

- [Jesus said,] **"On judgment day, many will say to me, 'Lord! Lord! We prophesied in your name and cast out demons in your name and performed many miracles in your name.' But I will reply, 'I never knew you. Get away from me, you who break God's law'"** (Matthew 7:22, 23, NLT).

4) Choosing to be proud instead of being humble

- [God says,] **"...I live in the high and holy place with those whose spirits are contrite and humble"** (Isaiah 57:15b, NLT).

- **"Then if my people who are called by my name will humble themselves and pray and seek my face and turn from their wicked ways, I will hear from heaven and will forgive their sins and restore their land"** (2 Chronicles 7:14, NLT).

Verbalize your struggles & successes in these areas.

"I am the light of the world. He who follows Me shall not walk in darkness, but have the light of life" (John 8:12, NKJV).

1) Daily prayers & prayer for today's schedule

2) Believers *(Names of Government Leaders, 1 Tim. 2:2)*

-
-
-
-
-
-
-
-
-
-

3) Unbelievers & People Groups

-
-
-
-
-
-

Last People Groups to Be Reached with Hope

Laos	Hung	4459
Laos	Kate	724
Laos	Khua	3816
Laos	Kuan	3635
Laos	Laoseng	9534
Laos	Mlabri	31
Laos	Nguon	1992
Laos	O'du	317
Laos	Phunoi	51861
Laos	Pong	31124
Laos	Pouhoy	291
Laos	Samtao	3533
Laos	Sila	2574
Laos	Singmoon	6869
Laos	Sou	3053
Laos	Tai He	11642
Laos	Tai Khang	7270
Laos	Tai Laan	582
Laos	Tai Pao	4799
Laos	Tayten	427
Laos	Thae	3777
Laos	Tong	13324
Laos	Yoy	1455
Lebanon	Deaf Lebanese	20955
Lesotho	Deaf Mosotho	9157
Liberia	Deaf Liberians	14207
Libya	Deaf Libyans	35955
Libya	Sawknah	7841
Libya	Wadshili	2914

Libya	Zuara	53465
Lithuania	Deaf Lithuanians	16585
Luxembourg	Deaf Luxembourger	2081
Macedonia	Deaf Macedonians	10385
Madagascar	Deaf Malagasians	87738
Malawi	Deaf Malawians	61755
Malaysia	Deaf Malaysians	135561
Malaysia	Javanese	11487
Malaysia	Kedayan	75000
Malaysia	Kensiu	316
Malaysia	Lahanan	714
Malaysia	Lelak	449

Day 24: Vigilance in Leaning on Christ

Defend your prayer life! Prayers are hindered by...

5) Worry (King Hezekiah modeled for us a path of leaning on God in the midst of his people being threatened.)
   - **"After Hezekiah received the [threatening] letter from the messengers and read it, he went up to the Lord's temple and spread it out before the LORD" (Isaiah 37:14, NLT).**
6) Not being still
   - **"He says, 'Be still and know that I am God; I will be exalted among the nations, I will be exalted in the earth'" (Psalm 46:10, NLT).**

Verbalize your struggles & successes in these areas.

"Yes, I am the gate. Those who come in through me will be saved. They will come and go freely and will find good pastures" (John 10:9, NLT).

1) Daily prayers & prayer for today's schedule

2) Believers *(Names of Prisoners, Hebrews 13:3)*

-
-
-
-
-
-
-
-
-
-

3) Unbelievers & People Groups

-
-
-
-
-
-

Last People Groups to Be Reached with Hope

Maldives	Deaf Maldivans	1833
Mali	Bangi Me	2420
Mali	Dogon Kolum So	35136
Malta	Deaf Maltese	1960
Mauritania	Deaf Mauritanians	6208
Mauritania	Zenaga	7841
Micronesia	Carolinian	2948
Micronesia	Namonuito	966
Micronesia	Ngatik	608
Micronesia	Satawalese	499
Mongolia	Deaf Mongolians	13745
Morocco	Deaf Moroccans	156060
Mozambique	DeafMozambicans	91681
Myanmar	Deaf Myanmarese	259132
Nepal	Byangsi	5670
Nepal	Chhulung	1634
Nepal	Deaf Nepalese	160033
Nepal	Ghale, Northern	2050
Nepal	Jerung	2427
Nepal	Kutang Bhotia	1932
Nepal	Lumba-Yakkha	1518
Nepal	Nar-Phuba	590
Nepal	Thudam Bhotia	2283
Nepal	Tilung	385
Nepal	Tseku	6075
Netherlands Antilles	Deaf Dutch Antilleans	1094
New Caledonia	Ara	472

New Caledonia	Aragure	1596
New Caledonia	Aro	923
New Caledonia	Dubea	2354
New Caledonia	Fwai	1681
New Caledonia	Hameha	506
New Caledonia	Javanese	10893
New Caledonia	Kaldosh Euronesian	1218
New Caledonia	Kwenyi	3023
New Caledonia	Neku	336
New Caledonia	Nemi	1008
New Caledonia	Nyua-Bonde	2865
New Caledonia	Pinje	168
New Caledonia	Sirhe	51
New Caledonia	Tiri	1008
New Caledonia	West Uvean	3142
New Caledonia	Xaracuu	5881

Day 25: Vigilance in Leaning on Christ

Defend your prayer life! Prayers are hindered by...

7) Not seeking God for help
   - **"You do not have because you do not ask God" (James 4:2b, NLT).**

8) Not caring to pray for the needs of others
   - **"And so, from the day we heard, we have not ceased to pray for you..." (Colossians 1:9a, ESV).**

Verbalize your struggles & successes in these areas.

"I am the good shepherd. The good shepherd sacrifices his life for the sheep" (John 10:11, NLT).

1) Daily prayers & prayer for today's schedule

2) Believers *(Distressed Neighbors, James 1:27)*

-
-
-
-
-
-
-
-
-

3) Unbelievers & People Groups

-
-
-
-
-
-
-

Last People Groups to Be Reached with Hope

New Caledonia	Yalayu	2119
Nigeria	Baangi	19404
Nigeria	Deaf Nigerians	742699
Nigeria	Dulbu	338
Nigeria	Kamkam	5520
Nigeria	Kyangawa	21224
Nigeria	Maha	26498
Nigeria	Shani	563
Nigeria	Taura	4416
North Korea	Deaf North Koreans	113136
Norway	Deaf Norwegians	21927
Oman	Batahira	1194
Oman	Deaf Omanis	15614
Oman	Harsusi	1384
Oman	Hobyot	138
Oman	Jibbali	41321
Oman	Kumzari	4959
Oman	Luwati	15000
Pakistan	Deaf Pakistanis	29302
Pakistan	Dumaki	1290
Pakistan	Gowro	300
Pakistan	Lassi	13804
Pakistan	Rajkoti	19720
Pakistan	Ushojo	3037
Pakistan	Yidgha	6000
Panama	Deaf Panamanians	18087
Papua New Guinea	Deaf Papua New Guineans	25598

Paraguay	Emok	1300
Paraguay	Mataco	2600
Peru	Deaf Peruvians	144183
Peru	Isconahua	90
Peru	Mashco Piro	103
Portugal	Deaf Portuguese	50717
Portugal	Mirandesa	10000
Qatar	Deaf Qataris	4495
Russia	Akhwakh	6500
Russia	Archi	2000
Russia	Bagvalal	6500
Russia	Chamalal	9500
Russia	Ginukh	200
Russia	Godoberi	2900
Russia	Hunzib	2000

Day 26: Vigilance in Leaning on Christ

Defend your prayer life! Prayers are hindered by...

9) Refusing to pray together with others
   - **"For where two or three are gathered together in my name, there am I in the midst of them" (Matthew 18:20, KJV).**

10) Avoiding praying with diverse groups of believers
    - **"They all joined together constantly in prayer, along with the women and Mary the mother of Jesus, and with his brothers" (Acts 1:14, NIV).**

Verbalize your struggles & successes in these areas.

"I am the resurrection and the life. Anyone who believes in me will live, even after dying. Everyone who lives in me and believes in me will never ever die" (John 11:25, NLT).

1) Daily prayers & prayer for today's schedule

2) Believers *(Names of Church Leaders, 2 Cor. 1:11)*

-
-
-
-
-
-
-
-
-
-

3) Unbelievers & People Groups

-
-
-
-
-

Last People Groups to Be Reached with Hope

Russia	Karata	5000
Russia	Khwarshi	1000
Russia	Tindi	5000
Russia	Tsez	7000
Rwanda	Deaf Rwandans	41162
Samoa	Deaf Samoans	860
San Marino	Emiliano-Romagnolo	22889
Saudi Arabia	Deaf Saudi Arabians	146436
Saudi Arabia	Shahara	43120
Senegal	Deaf Senegalese	65786
Serbia	Deaf Serbians	47457
Singapore	Deaf Singaporeans	22742
Slovenia	Deaf Slovenians	9799
Solomon Is.	Deaf Solomon Islanders	2503
Somalia	Dabarre	33057
Somalia	Deaf Somalis	47773
Somalia	Garre	82642
Somalia	Jiiddu	28515
Somalia	Mushungulu	28515
Somalia	Tunni	33057
South Sudan	Adja	291
South Sudan	Atwot	65974
South Sudan	Banda-Banda	4061
South Sudan	Banda-Mbres	10836
South Sudan	Banda-Ndele	22693
South Sudan	Bari Bai	3501

South Sudan	Dongotono	1061
South Sudan	Indri	980
South Sudan	Lango	41955
South Sudan	Lopit	70012
South Sudan	Ngalgulgule	1211
South Sudan	Thuri	20006
Spain	Fala	10500
Sri Lanka	Deaf Sri Lankans	87271
St. Lucia	Deaf Saint Lucians	812
Sudan	Baygo	1960
Sudan	Binga	1400
Sudan	Dair	1400
Sudan	Dar Fur Daju	98017
Sudan	Deaf Sudanese	214848
Sudan	Dgik	81289
Sudan	El Hugeirat	1428

Day 27: Vigilance in Leaning on Christ

Defend your prayer life! Prayers are hindered by…

11) Fasting in order to be seen by others rather than to focus on God
- **"When you fast, do not look somber as the hypocrites do for they disfigure their faces to show others they are fasting. Truly, I tell you, they have received their reward in full. But when you fast, put oil on your head and wash your face" (Matthew 6:16, 17, NLT).**

12) Avoiding fasting for church leaders
- **"So when they had appointed elders in every church, and prayed with fasting, they commended them to the Lord in whom they had believed" (Acts 14:23, ESV).**

Verbalize your struggles & successes in these areas.

"I am the way, the truth, and the life. No one can come to the Father except through me" (John 14:6, NLT).

1) Daily prayers & prayer for today's schedule

2) Believers *(Local Outreach Leaders, 2 Thess. 3:1)*

-
-
-
-
-
-
-
-
-
-

3) Unbelievers & People Groups

-
-
-
-
-
-

Last People Groups to Be Reached with Hope

Sudan	Eliri	4919
Sudan	Fa-c-Aka	3903
Sudan	Fanya	48394
Sudan	Fertit	11589
Sudan	Fongoro	1294
Sudan	Fungor	3757
Sudan	Ingessana	97802
Sudan	Kamdang	4201
Sudan	Kanga	12682
Sudan	Kara	280
Sudan	Karko	18547
Sudan	Keiga	17906
Sudan	Keiga Jirru	1960
Sudan	Kufa-Lima	15219
Sudan	Lafofa	7197
Sudan	Logol	3641
Sudan	Masakin	48193
Sudan	Midob	72841
Sudan	Mima	100940
Sudan	Molo	140
Sudan	Tagale	114704
Sudan	Tagoy	18567
Sudan	Talodi	2100
Sudan	Tese	1960
Sudan	Tima	1571
Sudan	Tingal	10982
Sudan	Togole	45324
Sudan	Tulishi	11615
Sudan	Tumale	2200

Sudan	Tumtum	10426
Sudan	Wali	1346
Sudan	Wali	52775
Sudan	Warnang	1571
Sudan	Yulu	4922
Suriname	Deaf Surinamers	2484
Swaziland	Deaf Swazis	6080
Sweden	Ingrian-Finns	300
Sweden	Swedish Travellers	25000
Sweden	Tattare Gypsies	25000
Switzerland	Deaf Swiss	38540
Syria	Deaf Syrians	104847
Syria	Lomavren	466180
Tajikistan	Aimaq	7762
Tajikistan	Parya	3000
Tanzania	Deaf Tanzanians	232722
Tanzania	Ndonde	17687

Day 28: Vigilance in Leaning on Christ

Defend your prayer life! Prayers are hindered by...

13) Avoiding fasting for missionaries
- **"While they were worshiping the Lord and fasting, the Holy Spirit said, 'Set apart for me Barnabus and Saul for the work to which I have called them'" (Acts 13:2, NIV).**

14) Avoiding a fast which focuses on helping the poor and oppressed
- **"If you spend yourself in behalf of the hungry and satisfy the needs of the oppressed, then your light will rise in the darkness, and your night will become like the noonday" (Isaiah 58:10, NIV).**

Verbalize your struggles & successes in these areas.

"Yes, I am the vine; you are the branches. Those who remain in me, and I in them, will produce much fruit. For apart from me you can do nothing" (John 15:5, NLT).

1) Daily prayers & prayer for today's schedule

2) Believers *(Global Outreach Leaders, Ephesians 6:19)*

-
-
-
-
-
-
-
-
-
-
-
-
-
-
-

Last People Groups to Be Reached with Hope

Tanzania	Pimbwe	51744
Tanzania	Segeju	18360
Tanzania	Vinza	19380
The Bahamas	Deaf Bahamians	1562
The Gambia	Deaf Gambians	9005
Timor Leste	Adabe	1294
Timor Leste	Kairui-Midik	2000
Timor Leste	Waimaha	5968
Tunisia	Deaf Tunisians	51887
Tunisia	Ghadames	2978
Tunisia	Tmagourt	7122
Uganda	Mening	6462
Uganda	Nubian	24965
United Arab Emirates	Deaf Emirians	17467
United Kingdom	Parsee	75000
United Kingdom	Scottish Travellers	4000
United States	Brunei	699
United States	Khuen	3042
United States	Mokilese	466
Vanuatu	Aore	13
Vanuatu	Deaf Ni-Vanuatuans	1318
Vanuatu	Vao	2519
Vanuatu	Wusi-Kerepua	402
Venezuela	Mandahuaca	3000
Venezuela	Mapoyo	365
Vietnam	Chut	6022

Vietnam	Gelao	2100
Vietnam	Pubiao	687
Vietnam	Red Tai	163340
Vietnam	Romam	436
Vietnam	Sila	709
Vietnam	Tsun-Lao	15396
West Bank	Deaf Palestinians	20699
West Bank	Samaritans	798
Yemen	Deaf Yemenis	97000
Yemen	Hobyot	29851
Zambia	Deaf Zambians	50047

Small Group Summary: The War Plan for Leaning on our Beloved Savior and King

To lean on Christ is to take up **"the shield of faith" (Ephesians 6:16)** in your war to abide in Christ. The following are some suggestions for leaning on our Beloved Savior and King:

Small Group Activities:

- **Adapt one of the verses above to a humorous skit. Have one person exemplify the good path, and the other person attempt to persuade the first against it.**
- **As a small group, discuss the verses above that have helped you in your prayer life and the verses that challenge you.**

Personal Activities:

- **Find a time to meet with God alone. Perhaps you can pair this with an early morning cup of coffee.**
- **Make every meeting with other believers into a prayer meeting. Perhaps you can plan to pray with them at the end of your time together.**
- **Find a time to have a fast from solid foods and have a "juice day". Perhaps this can be a couple of meals a week, when you need to make an important decision (see Acts 14:23), or when someone is sick (see Psalm 35:13).**

Be encouraged by the following verse: **"…[God] rewards those who earnestly seek him"** (Hebrews **11:6, NIV).** I am persuaded that Jesus Himself is our reward. Protect your relationship with Christ through leaning on Him for everything.

Juice Day Notes

For the remainder of the month, take some time to fast (health permitting), schedule the events for the upcoming month, coordinate schedules with your household, and pray through your schedules together. If your children want to fast with you, consider having a "Juice Morning" to fast and pray together. Instruct them to write down the verses that God brings to mind.

-
-
-
-
-
-
-
-
-
-
-
-
-
-
-
-
-

-
-
-
-
-
-
-
-
-
-
-
-
-
-
-
-
-
-
-
-
-
-
-
-

-
-
-
-
-
-
-
-
-
-
-
-
-
-
-
-
-
-
-
-
-
-
-
-
-

-
-
-
-
-
-
-
-
-
-
-
-
-
-
-
-
-
-
-
-
-
-
-

Appendix 1: Sample Bible Study

Below is a three-step plan for reading the Bible, which includes reading, repenting, and retelling.

1) Read

To have a consistent morning Bible time, I pair a positive (coffee) with a negative (waking up early). I anchor my morning Bible reading with good coffee.

- **Bible Highlighting Activity**
  i. Read a small portion of Psalms or the New Testament (about 10 verses). For practice, read the passage below and follow the steps:

Psalm 117:1, 2 (NLT)

Praise the LORD, all you nations.

Praise him, all you people of the earth.

For his unfailing love for us is powerful;

the LORD's faithfulness endures forever. Praise the LORD!

  ii. **"God did not give us a cowardly spirit, but a spirit of power, love…" (2 Timothy 1:7a, GWT).** Using a colored pencil, <u>highlight</u> where you find God's <u>love</u> displayed. <u>Underline</u> where you see God's <u>power</u> displayed.

iii.   **"God did not give us a cowardly spirit, but a spirit of … good judgment" (2 Timothy 1:7, GWT).** Using a colored pencil, <u>draw greater than and less than signs < … ></u> around verses that display the good path. <u>Draw bullet points</u> before and after verses ●…●that display the bad path.

2) **Repent**

Every Bible reading time is an opportunity to sit at our Beloved King's feet and listen to His teaching and discover His kindness. His kindness, in turn, leads us to repentance **(Romans 2:4)**. According to one Bible translation (the New Century Version), repentance means, "to change your heart and mind."

- **Bible Marking Activity**
  i.   Reread the passage of Psalms or the New Testament and ask yourself three questions: Where do I have to change my attitudes, beliefs, or actions.
  ii.   <u>Write</u> a lower case "**a**" in the column next to a verse that describes an **attitude** you need to change in your life. <u>Write</u> a lower case "**b**" next to a verse that describes a **belief** you need to change in your life. <u>Write</u> an upper case "**A**" next to a verse that describes an **action** that you need to change in your life.
  iii. Take an index card and write down one or two verses that you want to memorize. Practice

saying it five times aloud with the reference. Then say it without looking at the index card.

3) Retell

Find one or two others with whom you can study the same passage. Sharing with believers first is really good practice for sharing your faith with those who haven't heard the Gospel.

- **Bible Sharing Activity**
  i. Share the verses you have highlighted,
  ii. Share the verses that pertain to your repentance, and
  iii. Share also the verses that you are memorizing.

About the author:

Rev. William Hernandez serves with Healing Lamplight Pathway (a church plant with the Puget Sound Baptist Association) as Pastor and Prayer Advocate for Hidden and Hurting People Worldwide. He earned a bachelor's degree from UC Berkeley, a master's degree from Golden Gate Baptist Theological Seminary, and a doctorate from Trinity Theological Seminary. He and his wife and eight children serve in Europe, the Middle East, and North Africa.

33463117R00084